Words

Mike Wade

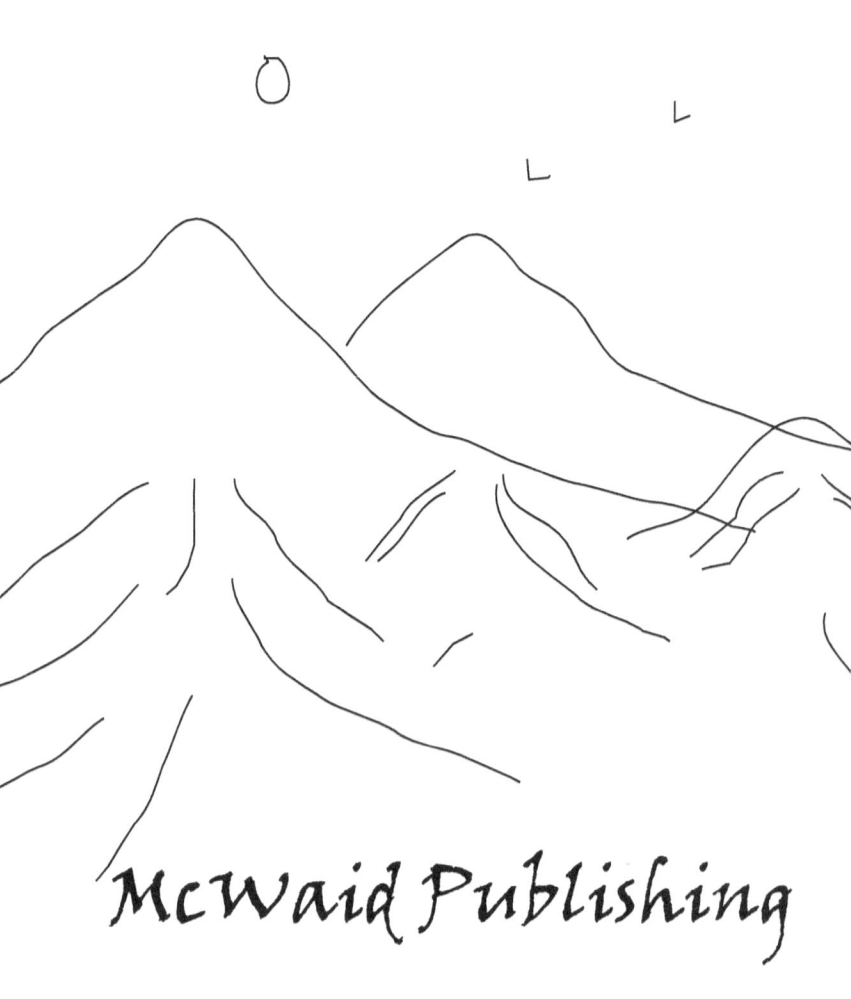

McWaid Publishing

Copyright © 2017 Mike Wade

All Rights Reserved

Write

To discover

To cry

To heal

To inspire

Just write!

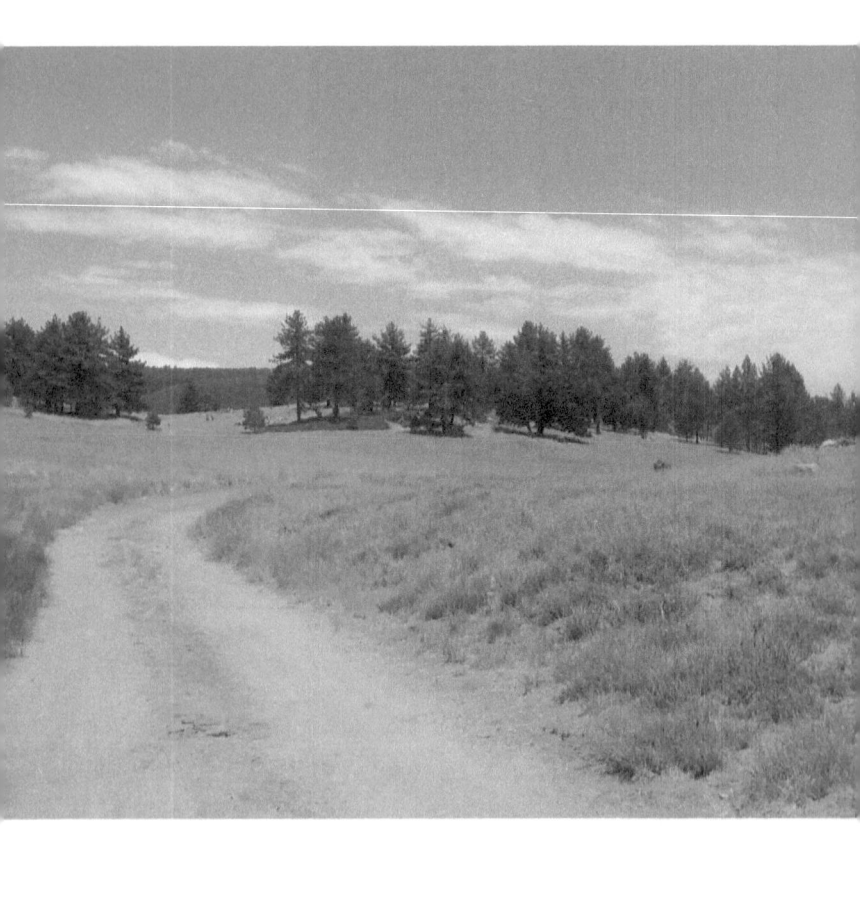

Connection

When my thoughts crawl back into

the caves of self-defeat

When solitude fades and isolation

appears to have claimed the victory

When purpose for living seems to

be disappearing in the wind

I stop

I turn down the chatter running

through my brain

I step back into the moment

I once again look beyond my

own walls of shame

I see your eyes

I find truth in your tears

I see your smile, I hear your laughter

I find Serenity when I connect

with your spirit within

Time stands still

My retreat loses its hold as sanity returns

It is you

It is I

It is us

Here lies the purpose

The meaning

The reason for each breath we take

For each step we walk.

So when this life has had its last say

may the path we have traveled

been lined with the gift of connection

May we find peace in knowing

that in the life we lived

We learned

We never had to walk alone

Santa Ysabel

Birds fly

all directions

They find their home

Mother Mary stands in guard

blessing their flight

My travels have been this

Not knowing my home

In flight, without a nest

Santa Ysabel was meant to be

Peace comes through the

eyes of the flock.

No more doubt

My path has been settled

From above, clarity has founds its place within

Meadow

Little tree in the middle of a field

telling me just how I feel

Especially those times when I just can't tell

Think I'll hang out for a spell

Ancestry

There are many rocks

on my path that were

there before I was born

I wish I had a bulldozer

to clear them away once

and for all

I just have a pick and shovel

to clear the way with each

step forward I go

Journey

Walk among the Pines, dance under the stars

The gates of heaven just don't seem that far

Life has been a mystery, a puzzle waiting to be solved

The years do paint a journey of transition

Finding serenity with the things that could change

making peace with what could not

In the moments yet to come

may solitude walk with connection

May the inner spirit be the guide

finding resolution with what lies beyond

Detached

I walked into the room

just had to assume

you'd be waiting too

Sat down on my chair

once again

lost in my delusions

Seasons change

Story remains the same

Rooms full of laughter

The silence is deafening

Can't find a way to

share the pain of despair

A Walk in the Woods

This path guards my every step

The sun welcomes my shadow

The silence stills my soul

This path brings solitude with connection to creation

A gift from above that lives within

This path moves beyond so many lost moments

Making peace with the days left behind

This path brings the pain of grief

Healing through tears

The promise of purpose

This path leads to this moment

Letting go of physical decline

Embracing spiritual rebirth

This path has found its beginning

Mysteries yet to unfold

Regression

In the distance

Watching

democracy pass

me by

Looking Into the

eyes of darkness

Missing the freedom

I didn't

realize I had

Total Eclipse

A moment of perfection

Humans conduct an investigation

Looking for a revelation

The heavens smile down in elation

Mankind unites, looking past its own finite creation

Eyes of a Cat

Simon in the morning

Subtle anticipation of moments
in silent connection

She welcomes the touch of
those who know love

Every sound awakens her senses
Mysteries waiting to be solved

As the sun sets, she finds
comfort in my return

Leaving the day behind
we sit side by side, watching the
stars bring life to a darkened sky

As I drift into sleep, Simon guards
my path against the monsters in
the closet that sometimes still take hold

Simon in the morning

Memories that shall forever paint
rainbows deep within my soul

Haiku

Friendship without pain

Memory lives in my brain

Just can't find your grave

Highway eighty four

Miles traveled back and forth

Passage through the Gorge

Societies game

Every battle is a loss

Seek without within

Love a windy day

Dance without thought or reason

Outcome left to chance

Tiny little roads

Where I am I just don't know

Confusion within

Sherwood forest bound

Leaving the nonsense behind

Healing quietly

Been a long road back

Tripping over my dusty tracks

Still hide behind mask

Birds sing to the trees

My own Shangri-La

Hood River dreaming

Perception within

Choice is becoming a gift

Captivity fades

Option of slow death

Suicide within living

Time to cut the loop

Among moonlit souls

Walking into the unknown

Walls of shame crumble

Setting sun behind

Spokane August on the run

Road without an end

Freeway at midnight

Los Angeles reflections

Still traveling home

Green leaves, spring it seems

Mild rains fall, hope is refined

Seeds sowed, path defined

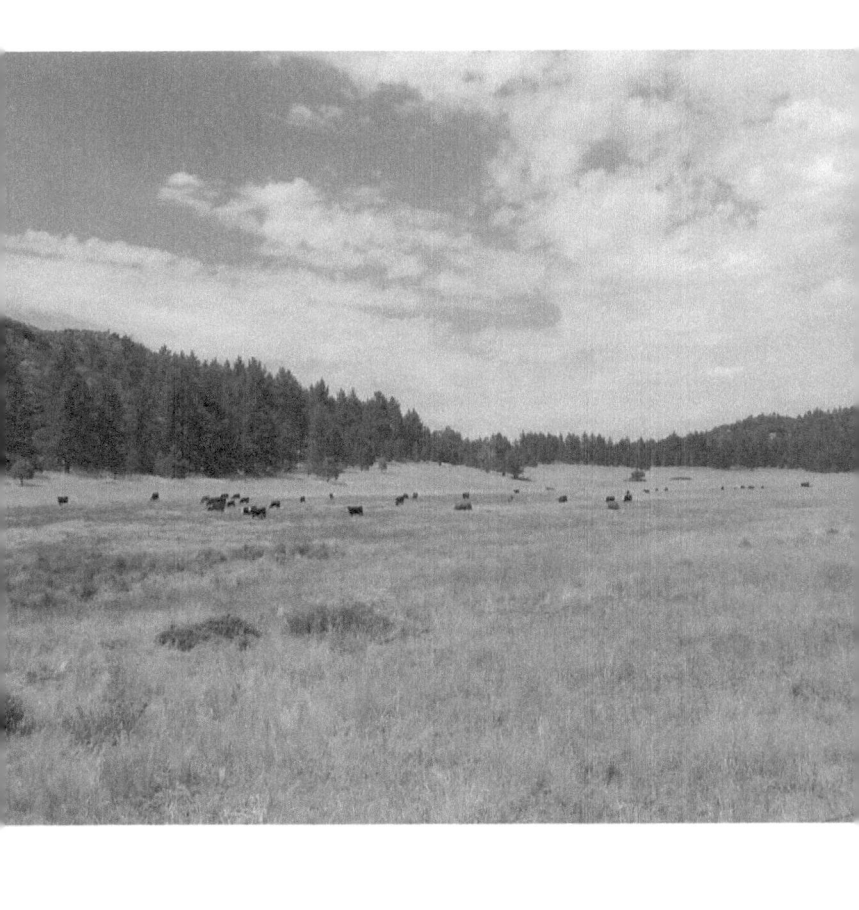

www.ingramcontent.com/pod-product-compliance
Lightning Source LLC
Chambersburg PA
CBHW031514210526
45464CB00007B/2912